volume

3

NAOKI URASAWA

Chapter 17 ● A Slight Possibility

UM... WHAT'S THAT?

HUH?

Chapter 17 ○ A Slight Possibility

ASADORA!

National Museum of
Nature and Science
Ueno, 1964

OH, *THIS* PHOTO-GRAPH?

THAT'S BECAUSE YOU RAN FROM ME!

NOW RETURN IT!

YES! IT'S IMPORTANT, SO GIVE IT BACK!

YOU ACT LIKE I *STOLE* IT.

IT COULD EASILY DESTROY A—

ITS CLAWS MUST'VE BEEN SHARP.

WERE THE GASHES IN THIS TREE...

...CAUSED BY A BEAR OR SOMETHING?

NO-BODY?

A NOBODY LIKE YOU WOULDN'T UNDERSTAND!!

I SAID GIVE THAT BACK!

IS THIS RESEARCH? THE WHITE COAT GIVES IT AWAY. YOU MUST BE A GREAT SCHOLAR!

THAT'S OKAY. I REALLY AM A NOBODY.

OOPS. S-SORRY.

8

...

?

IS THERE A CREATURE OUT THERE BIGGER THAN THAT ONE?

W...

OF COURSE THERE ISN'T!

...!!

WHY WOULD YOU ASK SUCH A THING?!

GIMME THOSE! THEY'RE IMPORTANT!

AGH!!

UM, I JUST—

A GIANT CREATURE?!

HEY, UH...

I'M SICK OF THAT TOPIC!!

HEY, YOU MISSED SOME!

AN UNIDENTIFIED LIFE-FORM?!

REAL-LY?

YES, AND THERE'S A LOT MORE.

WOW! THIS IS ALL RESEARCH?

I ONLY PUT IT THERE TO HELP MOVE THINGS ALONG SINCE YOU TOLD ME TO CLEAR OUT IMMEDIATELY!

OKAY, OKAY...

!!

I KNEW IT WAS YOU, NAKAIDO! YOU CAN'T PARK THAT CART IN FRONT OF THE MUSEUM!

I GOT THIS JOB RIGHT AFTER LOSING MY LAST OFFICE, SO I MOVED EVERYTHING HERE.

OKAY, OKAY.

WELL, DO IT THROUGH THE BACK!

THAT'S TOO BAD...

I'M ALWAYS GETTING KICKED OUT!

OH...

BUT NOW THAT THE JOB IS DONE, I HAVE TO LEAVE!

CREAK

WHOA...

THAT WON'T BE NECESSARY!

A NOBODY LIKE YOU HAS NO BUSINESS TOUCHING THIS STUFF!

THERE'S NO WAY YOU CAN CARRY ALL THIS ALONE.

I'LL LEND YOU A HAND.

FINE, I'M LEAVING.

UM, I'M SORRY!

YOU SAID IT AGAIN.

OOPS.

YOU SAID NO CREATURES BIGGER THAN THAT DINOSAUR EXIST...

...ABOUT MY QUESTION...

BUT...

HUH?

14

...

...BUT HOW CAN YOU BE SURE?

...IT'S UNKNOWN TO SCIENCE.

WELL, BECAUSE...

IF THERE'S EVEN A SLIGHT POSSIBILITY, IT'D BE WORTH LOOKING INTO.

BUT ISN'T THERE A POSSIBILITY?

GOOD-BYE.

YOU SOUND LIKE MY MENTOR.

...THIS MOUNTAIN OF RESEARCH.

YOUR MENTOR?

HE DIED AND LEFT BEHIND...

I SHOULDN'T BE TELLING THIS TO A NOBODY LIKE YOU.

SOR-RY.

I'M SICK OF IT...

...BUT I CAN'T GET RID OF IT.

SORRY! I DID IT AGAIN!

BOW

A GIANT CREATURE, HUH?

MISTER KA-SUGA?

GET IN.

IT'S LATE. WHERE'VE YOU BEEN?

THAT'S NOT WHERE WE'RE HEAD-ING.

NO THANKS. I'LL WALK HOME.

WHERE'VE *YOU* BEEN, MISTER?

JUST GET IN.

COMING BY CAR WAS A MISTAKE.

THIS TRAFFIC IS AWFUL.

SHE'D JUST TRY TO INTERFERE. WE'LL HANDLE HER LATER.

SHOULDN'T WE TELL KINUYO?

BUT THERE'S NO HURRY. WE CAN CATCH A LATE TRAIN.

IT'S ALL BECAUSE OF THE OLYMPICS.

TOKYO 1964

WELCOME OLYMPIC TEAMS

SO WE'RE TAKING...

HAMA-MATSU?

HAMA-MATSU.

AND THEN WHERE?

WE'RE GOING TO TOKYO STATION?

...THE HIKARI BULLET TRAIN?!

UGH... THIS IS THE SAME ONE WE TOOK WHEN WE LEFT NAGOYA FIVE YEARS AGO...

PLUS, I'M HUNGRY!

I'M SICK OF YOU DRAGGING ME AROUND.

WE MISSED IT AND THE KODAMA. THEY'D BE FULL ANYWAY.

THE HIKARI OPENED FOR SERVICE TODAY, YOU KNOW!

AWESOME!!

...A 150-YEN LUNCH!

OOH...

HERE! AN OPENING-DAY BOX LUNCH!

HEY,
WAKE
UP.

MUMBLE.
WHAT
TIME IS
IT?

IT'S
3 A.M.

HAMA-
MATSU...
HAMA-
MATSU...

UGH
...

IT'S
DAWN.

A JEEP?

?

WAIT HERE A MOMENT.

SKRIK

CHAK

WHERE ARE WE?

24

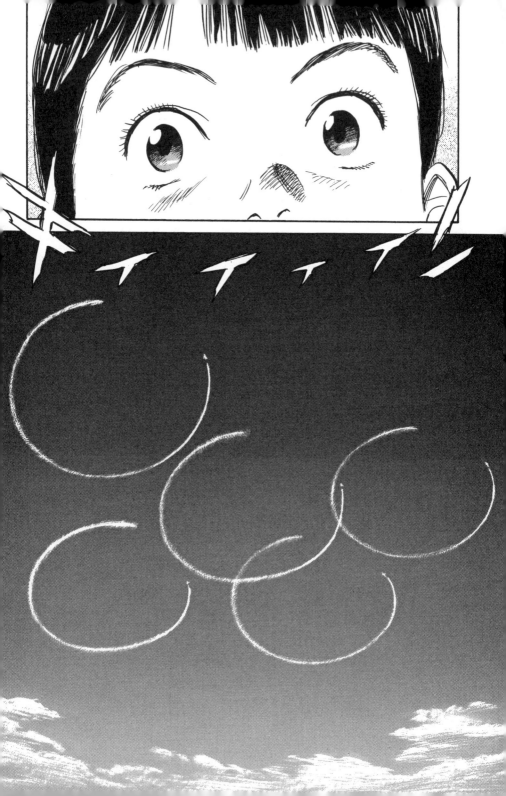

HERE
THEY
COME
AGAIN!

WHOA!

WOW!

THIS IS
GREAT!

Chapter 18 ◉ Five Rings

SKYWRITING NEVER FAILS TO AMAZE ME.

IT MUST TAKE SOME IMPRESSIVE FLYING.

HOW ARE THEY ABLE PULL OFF SOMETHING LIKE THAT?

HUH?

YES, BUT THEY HAVE YET TO SUCCEED.

DON'T YOU AGREE, MISTER?

THEY HAVE YET TO SUCCESSFULLY COMPLETE THE OLYMPIC SYMBOL.

UH...

WHAT'RE YOU TALKING ABOUT?!

IT'S PRACTICALLY IMPOSSIBLE TO EVEN PULL THAT MUCH OFF!

HUH?

ASA!

...BUT THEY STILL MADE THOSE RINGS! DO YOU KNOW HOW HARD THAT IS?!

THEY CAN BARELY SEE EACH OTHER UP THERE...

ASA!! DON'T TALK TO COLONEL JISSOJI LIKE THAT!!

BUT...

THAT'S ALL RIGHT.

I'M GLAD YOU KNOW HOW HARD IT IS.

?

WHEN IS THE ACTUAL PERFORMANCE?

THE OPENING CEREMONY IS OCTOBER 10.

THERE'S A DISTANCE OF 2.1 KILOMETERS BETWEEN EACH PLANE. EACH RING IS 1.8 METERS ACROSS. AND THE WHOLE DESIGN SPANS 6 KILOMETERS.

YOU'RE RIGHT.

...FOR IT TO BEGIN AT 1510 HOURS, 20 SECONDS.

THE ORGANIZING COMMITTEE HAS REQUESTED...

THAT'S AWFULLY PRECISE!

THAT'S IN ONE WEEK.

...AND THE RELEASE OF 10,000 DOVES...

AFTER THE ATHLETES' OATH...

...DIRECTLY IN FRONT OF THE ROYAL BOXES AT THE NATIONAL STADIUM.

...THE OLYMPIC RINGS MUST APPEAR...

THEY DON'T KNOW THE MEANING OF THE WORD.

B-BUT THAT'S IMPOSSIBLE!

IMPOSSIBLE?

AFTER ALL, THEY ARE *BLUE IMPULSE.*

THEN, IN 1958, AT A MEMORIAL CEREMONY HERE AT THE OPENING OF HAMAMATSU NORTH AIR BASE...

JAPAN WAS FORBIDDEN FROM PERFORMING AERIAL MANEUVERS FOR SEVEN YEARS FOLLOWING OUR DEFEAT IN WORLD WAR II.

...

...THREE F-86 SABRES ASTOUNDED SPECTATORS BY FLYING AEROBATIC MANEUVERS IN FORMATION.

...BUT I WAS ALREADY TOO OLD FOR A FIGHTER PLANE.

YES. I'D BEEN A HERO OF THE SKIES, SO IT WAS FRUSTRATING TO MERELY WATCH...

IT WAS HARD TO IMAGINE JAPANESE PILOTS EVER FLYING JET FIGHTERS AGAIN, BUT NOW...

DID YOU SEE IT?

THAT WAS ONE YEAR BEFORE WE MET.

IF I HAD FOUND YOU, I WOULD HAVE ASKED YOU TO PARTICIPATE.

AND INSTRUCTORS NEED TO BE ABLE TO SPEAK ENGLISH.

THANK YOU.

BUT THOSE WERE DARK DAYS FOR ME.

TUMP

ANYWAY, IT'S A NEW AGE.

...

...

JAPAN HAS COME A LONG WAY THESE PAST 19 YEARS.

NOW IT MUST MODERNIZE EVEN FURTHER.

TO ACCOMPLISH THAT GOAL, THE TOKYO OLYMPICS MUST SERVE AS A SYMBOL OF PEACE.

...WILL SIGNAL THAT.

THE RINGS INSCRIBED BY BLUE IMPULSE...

SO THEY MUST NOT FAIL.

HM?

WOW, COOL...

...GOOD-NESS!

OH MY...

TUMP

TUMP

TUMP

THE NEXT REHEARSAL IS TOMORROW IN TOKYO.

ERM...

YES, SIR! WE WON'T LET YOU DOWN!

BLUE IMPULSE, THE SECOND SQUADRON OF THE FIRST AIR WING, IS ALSO KNOWN AS THE TECHNICAL RESEARCH SECTION.

HUMF!

TUMP

40

...EVEN THE BEST PILOTS...

BUT...

THEY'RE ELITE PILOTS SELECTED FROM THE MOST ADEPT INSTRUCTORS.

YES. TEN AMERICAN FIGHTERS, TRANSPORT AIRCRAFT AND HELICOPTERS HAVE CRASHED THIS YEAR.

...SOMETIMES HAVE TROUBLE.

THE PILOT ESCAPED UNHARMED, BUT FOUR CIVILIANS DIED AND 32 SUFFERED SEVERE INJURIES.

ON APRIL 5, AN AMERICAN F-8U NAVY FIGHTER HEADING TO NAVAL AIR STATION ATSUGI EXPERIENCED TROUBLE OVER MACHIDA, TOKYO, AND CRASHED.

LAST MONTH, ON SEPTEMBER 8, AN AMERICAN NAVAL FIGHTER CRASHED AFTER TAKEOFF AT ATSUGI.

AGAIN, THE PILOT ESCAPED, BUT THE SURROUNDING HOMES AND A FACTORY WERE COMPLETELY DESTROYED, KILLING FIVE WORKERS AND SEVERELY INJURING THREE.

...THE AIRCRAFT WILL BE FLYING OVER DENSELY POPULATED TOKYO.

AND THIS TIME...

...

TO PREVENT INJURING CIVILIANS...

PERMIT?

SO THE PILOTS WILL NOT PERMIT SUCH AN ACCIDENT.

INSTEAD, THEY WILL AIM FOR THE SEA...

...OR A RIVER, MOUNTAIN OR SWAMP...

...THE PILOTS CAN'T SIMPLY BAIL OUT.

...EVEN IF IT MEANS THEIR DEATH.

...THEY BEAR A HEAVY BURDEN.

THEN...

THAT'S WHY I NEED *YOUR* HELP.

HUH?

YOU WANT *ME* TO DO THE SKYWRITING?!

M-ME?

DON'T GET COCKY! YOU'VE NEVER EVEN PILOTED A FIGHTER!

THAT HURT...

I MEAN, I THINK SO, BUT—

BUT CAN I PULL IT OFF?

OW!!

44

IS THIS WHAT YOU BELIEVE YOU SAW?

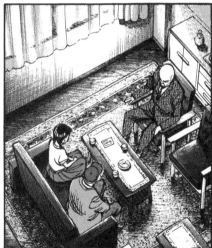

YES.

YOUR FAMILY DIED IN THE ISEWAN TYPHOON.

NO...

KASUGA TOLD ME ABOUT IT.

...IS ALIVE SOME-WHERE.

MY FAMILY...

...

...TOOK THEM AWAY.

BUT THIS THING...

46

...THIS IS FINALLY COMING TO LIGHT.

SO I'M GLAD...

NOW WE KNOW IT'S REAL.

AND THE SELF-DEFENSE FORCES WILL TAKE ACTION!

...AND FIND MY FAMILY!!

PLEASE, YOU GOTTA BEAT THAT THING...

AS I MENTIONED...

...THE OLYMPICS ARE A CELEBRATION OF *PEACE*.

BESIDES...

WE MUST SHOW THE WORLD THAT JAPAN HAS BEEN REBORN.

...

...WE DON'T EVEN KNOW WHAT *THIS* IS.

FURTHER-MORE...

...THE CONSTITUTION STRICTLY REGULATES USE OF THE SDF.

EVEN IF THIS IS THE THREAT YOU BELIEVE YOU SAW...

...THE ARMED FORCES CANNOT ACT.

ASADORA!

ASADORA!

WHAT FOR?

Chapter 19 ◉ Things You Can't Say

TO, ERM, YOU KNOW...

WELL, UM... TO...

FOR WHAT PRODUCT?

...ABOUT TRAILING AN ADVERTISEMENT BANNER!

W-WE HAD A MEETING...

UM...

EEL!

...

YEAH, RIGHT! A LONG EEL!

ASA! WEREN'T YOU LISTENING?!

EEL?!

THE BANNER'LL LOOK LIKE A LOOOOONG EEL.

Y-YEAH, EEL.

...

I KNOW THE COMPANY IS IN TROUBLE...

...AND YOU'RE IN DANGER OF LOSING THE PLANE.

HOW-EVER!

Y-YES, MA'AM.

I'M FILLING IN FOR YOUR MOTHER AS GUARDIAN!

ASA NEEDS *MY* PERMISSION FOR OVERNIGHTS...

...AND SCHOOL ABSENCES!!

AND SOME- DAY...

YOU, HAZUKI, SHINROKU AND KOSHICHI ARE IMPORTANT TO HER *AND* ME.

KINUYO ...

...I'M GIVING YOU BACK.

...AFTER YOU'VE GROWN UP...

I INTEND TO TEACH YOU TO VALUE YOUR LIVES.

...BUT I'M RESPONSIBLE FOR YOU.

I DON'T WANT TO BE OVER- PROTECTIVE...

KA-SUGA!

EEP!

THANK YOU.

I UNDER-STAND.

WELL SAID, KINUYO.

YES, INDEED...

AS I'VE SAID BEFORE...

ULP!

I DON'T CARE ABOUT YOU, BUT NOTHING MUST HAPPEN TO ASA!

THIS INVOLVES YOU TOO!

...

I ONLY ALLOW IT BECAUSE SHE'S OBSESSED WITH IT.

URM...

BUT IF ANYTHING HAPPENS, NO MORE!

...I'M AGAINST ASA FLYING THAT PLANE!

SHE'S REALLY MAD.

WHEW...

COME DOWN AND HELP. IT'S OPENING TIME.

TUNK TUNK

GUESS WE CAN'T TELL HER.

WE DEFINITELY CAN'T TELL HER...

NOPE.

...WHAT WE AGREED TO DO.

Hamamatsu North Air Base

...IF THIS THING IS ALIVE.

WE DON'T EVEN KNOW...

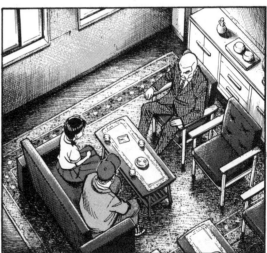

...THE UNITED STATES MIGHT SUSPECT...

FOR ALL WE KNOW...

YOU MEAN IT MIGHT NOT BE?

THE POINT IS, WE DON'T KNOW.

OH...

...THAT THIS IS A SECRET WEAPON DESIGNED BY THE COMMUNIST BLOC.

THAT'S WHY I NEED YOU, KASUGA.

CORRECT.

...I WANT YOU TO FLY CLOSE AND ASCERTAIN WHAT IT IS.

THE NEXT TIME THIS THING APPEARS...

...YOU MUST BE PREPARED FOR ANYTHING.

BUT SINCE IT'S AS-YET UNIDENTIFIED...

AT THE OPENING CEREMONY, BLUE IMPULSE MUST BE FLAWLESS...

YOU MEAN LIKE A FIGHT.

...AS THEY TRACE THE OLYMPIC RINGS...

YES. WHICH MEANS THE SDF MUST BE NOWHERE CLOSE.

...AS A SYMBOL OF PEACE.

HOW-EVER...

KASUGA, I ASKED YOU BECAUSE YOU ONCE HAD THE SKILLS TO EVADE DANGER.

AND THEN I ASKED...

...BUT I'M NOT THE "HERO OF THE SKIES" I WAS IN THE WAR.

I ANSWERED THAT I CAN STILL PERFORM REGULAR MANEUVERS DESPITE THE GUNSHOT WOUND TO MY ARM FIVE YEARS AGO...

...ABOUT YOUR BELOVED PUPIL.

AND I SAID...

I'VE RARELY SEEN ANYONE FLY LIKE HER.

...SHE CAN'T HACK IT.

HOW- EVER...

YES, I CAN! I—

...OUR PIPER J-3 CUB...

...HAS CONTROLS IN BOTH THE FRONT AND BACK...

...SO IF ANYTHING HAPPENS TO ME...

...SHE MIGHT COME IN HANDY.

WE HAVE ONE WEEK...

...UNTIL THE OLYMPIC OPENING CEREMONY.

DON'T GET COCKY.

YOU BET I WOULD!

ANYTHING COULD HAPPEN UNTIL THEN.

BE READY TO ACT AT A MOMENT'S NOTICE.

YES, SIR.

ASAAA!!

!!

...TO HELP OUT!

I...I'LL BE RIGHT THERE...

DEFINITELY CAN'T TELL KINUYO.

NOPE.

YOUR FRIEND NAKAJIMA.

NAKA-JIMA?

A CALL?

TUNK

TUNK TUNK

WHO'S IT FROM?

YOU HAVE A PHONE CALL.

YOU MISSED SCHOOL. ARE YOU SICK?

HELLO? ASA?

UH...HI, YONE!

A FAVOR?

WELL, GET BETTER. BY THE WAY, I HAVE A FAVOR TO ASK.

KOFF KOFF

I'M F-FINE! JUST A LITTLE COUGH!

I'M GOING TO GO.

YEAH, YOU SEE...

HUH? GO WHERE?

TO THE ENTER- TAINMENT AGENCY.

...HOLD ON A SECOND!

WHAT?! Y-YONE...

SHE WANTS TO MAKE HER DEBUT WITH YOU.

HAVE YOU TALKED TO MIYAKO ABOUT IT?

BUT—

...THE SCOUT SAID...

BUT...

REALLY! YOU SHOULD TALK TO HER!

UM...

HMM...

...HERE'S MY FAVOR...

SO...

...HE'S ONLY INTERESTED IN ME.

HUH
?!

I WANT
YOU TO
COME
WITH ME.

YEAH,
BUT...

I'D FEEL
BETTER IF
YOU WERE
THERE
WITH ME.

I'M
AFRAID
TO GO
ALONE...

...FOR
NEXT
FRIDAY,
OCTOBER
9.

I
MADE AN
APPOINT-
MENT...

UH,
WELCOME
TO
KINUYO'S!

RATTLE

WHAT?!
THE DATE'S
ALREADY
SET?!

YEAH, B-BUT...

THIS WAY, THERE'S NO CONFLICT!

WEL-COME, SIR!

YEAH! THE OLYMPICS START THE NEXT DAY!

SERIOUSLY?! HOLD ON, YONE!

DID YOU AT LEAST ASK YOUR PARENTS?

WE HAVE A CUS-TOMER!

OFF THE PHONE, ASA!

UH... RIGHT.

YONEKO! TIME FOR SUPPER!

HUH?

OKAY, I'M COM-ING!

HURRY UP! AFTER THAT, YOU HAVE HOMEWORK!

UH... RIGHT.

...TELL MY PARENTS.

I CAN'T...

...I UNDER-STAND.

YEAH...

...

OKAY!

ASA!

CHAK

...NEXT WEEK AT SCHOOL.

ANYWAY, LET'S TALK...

SIGH.

OKAY, BYE.

I'LL BRING A MOIST TOWEL!

WELCOME, SIR!

!!

OH, RIGHT!

WATER.

WHAT WOULD YOU LIKE TO DRINK?

HUH?

UH, SURE.

WATER.

THE, UH, MENU IS ON THE WALL.

もつ煮込 120円

揚出し豆腐 160

えび唐揚げ 180円

*MENU: SIMMERED GIBLETS ¥180, DEEP-FRIED TOFU ¥160, DEEP-FRIED SHRIMP ¥180

?

I COME AS A MESSENGER.

74

HUH?

MR. JISSOJI SENT ME. I AM A-KURA.

A-KURA?

WHAT?!

I WILL STATION MYSELF NEAR YOU TWO 24 HOURS A DAY.

...I WILL REQUIRE YOUR IMMEDIATE MOBILIZATION.

THE NEXT TIME *THAT THING* APPEARS...

SKRIK

THIS IS CLOSE ENOUGH.

IF YOU DO THAT, EVERYONE WILL NOTICE!

I MUST TAKE YOU TO THE SCHOOL ENTRANCE.

...

I AM A BODYGUARD AS WELL AS A MESSENGER.

YOU MAY BE TRYING TO KEEP A LOW PROFILE, BUT YOU REALLY STAND OUT, SO...

UM, MR. A-KURA?

...

Y-YOU'RE SO STUBBORN!

W-WHAT-EVER...

I WILL WAIT FOR YOU HERE AFTER SCHOOL.

*POLE: PAWN SHOP   DAIKOKUYA   ENTRANCE

HM?

SIGH.

質
大
黒
屋

入口

GYAAAH!!

SINCE WHEN DO YOU HAVE YOUR OWN DRIVER?!

AFTER I BECOME A FAMOUS ENTERTAINER...

DON'T STARE. LET'S GO, MIYAKO!

OH, REALLY?

TH-THAT'S JUST ONE OF KINUYO'S REGULARS. HE HAPPENED TO BE DRIVING BY AND, UM...

OH!

HI, GIRLS!

NEVER MIND THAT. COME ON!

...I'LL NEED A CAR LIKE THAT WHEN FANS SWARM ME!

HUH?

...

GOOD MORNING, YONE!

GOOD MORNING!

OF COURSE! IT'S ALWAYS SO FUNNY!

...

HEY, DID YOU WATCH *SHABONDAMA HOLIDAY* LAST NIGHT?

Chapter 20 ◉ The Search Begins

"IF ONLY YOUR MA WERE ALIVE TO DO THIS."

"KOFF! KOFF! THANKS..."

"HERE'S YOUR GRUEL, PA!"

THEN OSAMI NABE SAYS, "CUT! CUUUT!!"

WHAT'RE YOU GONNA DO?!

HUH?

YONE!

"YOU MUSTN'T SAY THAT, PA!"

HEY, GUESS WHAT?!

WHY SHOULD I DO IT?!

YOU TELL HER, ASA!

YOU GOTTA TELL HER ABOUT THE ENTERTAINMENT AGENCY!

HMM...

I RESERVED A COPY AT THE RECORD STORE. WHY DON'T YOU TWO COME WITH ME TO PICK IT UP?

THE BEATLES' NEW SONG "AND I LOVE HER" GOES ON SALE TODAY!

Y-YES?!

EEP!

Y-YEAH...

RECORD CONCERT?

YONE AND I WENT TO A BEATLES RECORD CONCERT JUST THE OTHER DAY!

CAN YOUR ALLOWANCE COVER THAT?

HUH? THEY RELEASE A NEW SONG EVERY MONTH.

BUT UNTIL OUR DEBUT, I GOTTA KEEP UP WITH THE SCENE.

ONLY BARELY!

IT WAS JUST LIKE WESTERN CARNIVAL AT NIHON GEKIJO!!

THE CONCERT HALL PLAYED BEATLES RECORDS AT TOP VOLUME AND THE GIRLS WENT WILD!!

PAUL

JOHN

GO ON. TELL HER.

YEAH...

HUH?

YOU TWO SHOULD LISTEN TO THE BEATLES TOO! ESPECIALLY YOU, ASA!

...PEOPLE WILL SWOON OVER US TOO!

ONCE WE MAKE OUR DEBUT...

IT'S "BECAUSE I LOVE YOU..." ♪

NO!

THE ONE THAT GOES "LOVE YOU OF COURSE" ♪

YOU ALWAYS SING THAT ONE SONG!

IT'S WAY BETTER THAN THAT DUMB SONG!

IT ISN'T DUMB!

NOPE.

DID YOU EVER FIGURE OUT WHO SINGS IT?

AFTER I PICK UP THE RECORD, LET'S LISTEN TO IT AT MY HOUSE!

DING DONG

I CAN'T BELIEVE YOU.

THEN TELL HER FOR ME.

IF YOU DON'T, IT'LL CAUSE TROUBLE LATER.

WELL...

YOU'RE NOT GOING TO TELL HER?

LET'S GO GET THAT RECORD!

ULP...

YOU TWO FINISHED UP QUICK IN THE RESTROOM!

THANKS FOR WAITIN'!

GYAH!

ASA HAS A DRIVER?

HEY, THERE'S YOUR DRIVER!

HE'S NOBODY! LET'S GO.

THERE'S BEEN A DEVELOP-MENT.

NO. I'M GOING TO A FRIEND'S HOUSE.

GET IN.

A DEVELOPMENT? REALLY?

YES.

...

I HAVE TO GO.

FORGIVE ME.

HUH?

SORRY.

I'LL JOIN YOU NEXT TIME.

HUH?

HOW COME?

KOFF!

KOFF!
KOFF!

GYAH!!

I DUNNO...

W-WHAT THE?

WHAT HAPPENED?!

...OR 20 MINUTES BY PLANE, SO TAKE ME TO...

THAT'S ABOUT 40 TO 50 KILO-METERS AWAY...

HUH?

...?

HAMA-MATSU? SHONAN? CHIBA?

WHERE DID IT APPEAR?!

HEY! THE AIRFIELD IS BACK THAT WAY!

SKRIK

HUH ...?

WHERE ARE WE?

W-WHAT'S GOING ON?

HUH?

THIS IS THE NEIGHBOR-HOOD.

HEY!

IT SHOULD BE AROUND HERE.

THIS IS THE RIGHT BLOCK, BUT...

MISTER KASUGA!

THEY CONTACTED ME TOO. WHAT'RE WE DOING HERE?

THIS IS A RED-LIGHT DISTRICT.

THIS IS NO PLACE FOR ASA!

A WHAT?

...INVOLVE HER IN THIS BUSINESS!

YOU BETTER NOT...

NO, IT JUST CHANGED FORM!

LET'S GO, ASA!

HUH?

THE RED-LIGHT DISTRICT DISAPPEARED SIX YEARS AGO.

THIS WAY. HURRY.

WHAT'S GOING ON HERE?

HERE'S THE OWNER.

WHOA...

I JUST OWN THE BUILDING. THAT'S ALL!

H-HELLO, I'M NORO.

AS YOU CAN SEE, NO ONE'S USING IT.

BUT IT USED TO BE A LIVELY DANCE HALL.

OKAY?

ACCORDING TO OUR INVESTIGATION, THERE'S SOMETHING HERE.

NOTHING IN-APPROPRIATE IS GOING ON HERE ANYMORE!

WHO ARE YOU PEOPLE?

INVESTI-GATION?!

LIKE WHAT?

...!!

HEY, NOT IN FRONT OF THE GIRL!

ALTHOUGH DANCE HALL CUSTOMERS DID USED TO GO UPSTAIRS FOR A LITTLE HANKY-PANKY.

...BUT THEN JAPAN GOT THE OLYMPICS.

FWIK

...AFTER THE ANTI-PROSTITUTION LAW PASSED, I PLANNED ON TURNING THE PLACE INTO A STRIP CLUB OR A CABARET...

KOFF! ANYWAY...

BUT THEN I THOUGHT...

THE GOVERNMENT'S BEAUTIFICATION PROJECT OR WHATEVER PUT AN END TO THAT REAL QUICK.

EVERYONE! CUZ THEY'VE ALL GOT DIRTY MINDS!

WHO'D WANNA SEE THAT?!

...I COULD MAKE A MUSEUM DEDICATED TO SEX PARAPHERNALIA FROM ALL TIMES AND PLACES!

I SAID NOT IN FRONT OF THE GIRL!

CREAK

CHAK

...YOU CAN LOOK AROUND, BUT YOU WON'T FIND ANYTHING ILLEGAL!

ANYWAY... KOFF...

ANYWAY, JUST KEEP WORKING.

MAYBE I CAN USE IT IN MY MUSEUM.

...MY COUSIN'S BOY DOES KEEP SOME WEIRD STUFF IN THERE.

HOW-EVER...

CREAK

YOU...

HEY!

?

YOU'RE
...

NO, YOU DON'T UNDER-STAND!

YOU KNOW HER, KEIICHI? YOU SMOOTH OPERATOR, YOU!

WHAT'RE *YOU* DOING HERE?!

W-WHAT ARE *YOU* DOING HERE?!

W...

AS A KID, HE WAS ONLY INTERESTED IN SNAKES AND FROGS, BUT I GUESS HE'S FINALLY TAKEN AN INTEREST IN WOMEN.

KEIICHI NAKAIDO. HE'S MY COUSIN'S BOY.

HIS NAME IS KEIICHI?

HUH?

YOU'RE MR. NAKAIDO, EH?

WHAT'RE YOU TALKING ABOUT?!

NO...IT ISN'T LIKE THAT!

AND *YOU'RE* THE ONE WHO FILCHED IT.

PROFESSOR SHINNOSUKE YODOGAWA WAS AN UNORTHODOX BIOLOGIST WHOSE RESEARCH WENT MISSING FROM THE UNIVERSITY.

YEAH! THAT'S WHY HE TOOK THIS STUFF!

...SO THE UNIVERSITY WANTED TO ERASE HIS LIFE'S WORK!

PROFESSOR YODOGAWA HAD A DODGY REPUTA-TION...

SEE IT?

DID YOU SEE IT?

WE MET AT THE SCIENCE MUSEUM IN UENO.

HOW DO *YOU* KNOW ALL THIS?

HUH?

PROFESSOR YODO-GAWA'S RESEARCH.

WHAT ARE WE TALKING ABOUT?!

W-WHAT?

KEIICHI! WHAT SORT OF VILE STUFF DID YOU BRING HERE?

HE WAS RESEARCHING *YOU-KNOW-WHAT.*

I EXPECT TO BE COMPEN-SATED FOR MY HELP!

STOP! YOU CAN'T JUST BARGE IN THERE!

TAK

TAK

TAK

WHAT?

...

HM? STORAGE IS THIS WAY...

WHERE'S THE RESEARCH?

IN HERE, WE WILL FIND...

...THE TRUTH OF THE MATTER!

ASADORA!

ASADORA!

*SIGN: DAILY MORNING NEWS SALES OFFICE

I'M GOING NOW!

HEY!

Y-YES?!

MY APOLO-GIES, SIR!

I'LL DO BETTER THIS TIME!

MESS UP YOUR DELIVERIES AGAIN, AND YOU'RE FIRED!

YOU GET SO CAUGHT UP IN *RUNNING* THAT YOU FORGET THE PAPERS!

I'M SORRY, SIR!

THIS MORNING I GOT FIVE CALLS ABOUT MISSING DELIVERIES!

ENOUGH! JUST GO!

I'M SOR-RY—

...HOW CAN YOU EXPECT TO MAKE THE OLYMPICS?!

IF YOU CAN'T EVEN DELIVER NEWSPAPERS RIGHT...

NOW GET GOING!

MAKE YOUR FATHER AND BROTHERS PROUD!

YES, ABOUT THAT...

WAIT, YOU GOT MAIL.

YOUR WIFE ALREADY GAVE IT TO ME!

OKAY! I'M OFF FOR DELIVERIES!

WAS THERE A PACKAGE AGAIN?

YES, EVERY TIME HE GETS A LETTER...

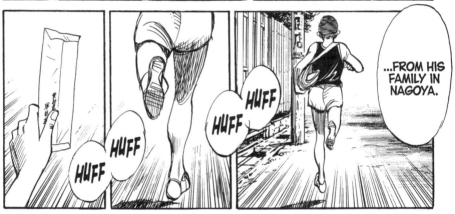

HUFF

HUFF

HUFF

HUFF

...FROM HIS FAMILY IN NAGOYA.

"DEAR SHOTA..."

Shota Hayata
c/o Mr. and Mrs. Sakurai,
Daily Morning News
Sales Office
Naka Town, Koganei City,
Tokyo

"I HOPE YOU AREN'T CAUSING ANY TROUBLE FOR MR. AND MRS. SAKURAI, WHO MUST RUN THE NEWSPAPER SALES OFFICE IN ADDITION TO TAKING CARE OF YOU."

"YOUR OLDER BROTHERS ARE AS HEALTHY AS EVER, SO DON'T WORRY ABOUT US!"

HUFF HUFF HUFF HUFF HUFF

HUFF HUFF HUFF HUFF

"WE SENT THEM A GIFT AS A TOKEN OF GRATITUDE."

"MAKE SURE YOU SAY THANK YOU EVERY DAY."

HUFF HUFF

"THANKS TO THE LETTER OF INTRODUCTION FROM THE FACTORY MANAGER IN NAGOYA, I (SHOJI) START WORK IN TOKYO NEXT MONTH."

HUFF HUFF

THREE CAKES... EVERY MONTH...

MORE OF NAGOYA'S FAMOUS UIRO...

MUNCH MUNCH

NOM NOM

*BOX: UIRO

I CAN DO IT! I CAN DO IT!

"JUST KEEP TELLING YOURSELF YOU CAN DO IT!"

I...

I CAN DO IT! I CAN DO IT!

"FOCUS ON TOMOR- ROW!"

WHEEZ

I...

HUFF WHEEZ

WHEEZ HUFF HUFF WHEEZ

WHEEZ HUFF

ASA...

OH NO!

GASP!

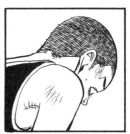

ACK! THAT'S THREE HOUSES!

YAMAMOTO, NAKANISHI AND KOKUBO!

I MISSED SOME DELIVERIES!

I GOTTA GO BACK AND—

WHSH

I THINK THAT'S HIM...

I'D KNOW THAT FORM ANY- WHERE.

I ONCE SAW HIM FROM A DISTANCE AT AN OLYMPIC QUALIFYING RACE.

THAT'S *KOKICHI TSUBURAYA!!*

WHAT AM I STANDING AROUND HERE FOR?!

...!!

...

THIS IS MY CHANCE TO RACE...

...A WORLD-CLASS RUNNER!

...TO RUN WITH A GUY FROM THE NATIONAL TEAM!

I CAN'T MISS THIS OPPOR-TUNITY...

I WONDER WHAT THE OLYMPIC MARATHON IS LIKE!

WELL, HE CAN SHOW ME!

NO, I'M...

H-HE'S FAST!

SHOULD I DITCH THE NEWSPAPERS?

I'M HEAVY!!

...

"I HOPE YOU AREN'T CAUSING ANY TROUBLE FOR MR. AND MRS. SAKURAI, WHO MUST RUN THE NEWSPAPER SALES OFFICE IN ADDITION TO TAKING CARE OF YOU."

ARGH!

UMPH!

EXTRA WEIGHT IS GOOD FOR TRAINING!

DAD, SHOICHI, SHOJI...

I'M IN TOKYO AND...

...DIDN'T MAKE THE NATIONAL TEAM, BUT...

I KNOW I LET EVERY- ONE DOWN WHEN I...

...I'M RUNNING AGAINST KOKICHI TSUBURAYA!

HM?

WHAT THE?

I CAN'T BELIEVE IT!

NO WAY...

I'M CLOSING IN!!

NO, IT
ISN'T!

IS
IT MY
IMAGI-
NATION?

I'M
GAINING
ON HIM!

OF COURSE,
JAPAN'S BEST
CHANCES FOR
MEDALS IN
THE OLYMPIC
MARATHON ARE
KENJI KIMIHARA
AND TORU
TERASAWA, WHO
HAS JAPAN'S
FASTEST TIME.

KOKICHI
TSUBURAYA'S
RISE TO THE
TEAM AFTER
JUST THREE
MARATHONS
WAS
METEORIC,
BUT...

...I'M
GONNA
PASS
HIM!

...I
THINK...

BUT...

EVEN WITH ALL THESE HEAVY NEWSPAPERS!

ASA!

"I SAW THE NAMES OF JAPAN'S OLYMPIC MARATHON RUNNERS IN THE NEWS."

"DEAR SHO,

HOW HAVE YOU BEEN? I HOPE YOU GET THIS LETTER."

"THE SHO I KNOW IS AN OUTSTANDING RUNNER."

"TO BE HONEST, I WAS RELIEVED. AFTER ALL, YOU'RE GOING TO GET MUCH FASTER, SO IT WOULD BE A WASTE IF YOU COMPETED NOW."

"EVERYONE IN TOKYO IS TREATING ME WELL. I'M SURE IT'S THE SAME FOR YOU."

"HE TRAINS HARD EVERY DAY AND NEVER COMPLAINS. AND HE'S A NICE GUY WHO PUTS OTHERS BEFORE HIMSELF."

"WRITE ME WHEN YOU CAN.

—ASA"

"EVEN AWAY FROM NAGOYA, YOU'RE A RAY OF HOPE."

ASA!

*SIGNS: PINK SPOT SALON, EL DORADO, BLACK ROSE

YES?

ASA?

YES.
ASA
ASADA.

YOUR
NAME IS
ASA?

"ASA..."

BORING, HUH? IT MEANS "MORN-ING"...

...BECAUSE THAT'S WHEN I WAS BORN.

N-NO, UH...

DELUSIONAL? BUT YOU SAW THE PHOTO!

I'M NOT A REAL SCHOLAR YET, BUT YES, THEY CONTAIN PROFESSOR YODOGAWA'S DELUSIONAL THEORIES.

...IT'S NOT BORING.

HEY, SCHOLAR. ARE ALL THESE PAPERS ABOUT *YOU-KNOW-WHAT?*

...AS PROOF THAT HIS PERSISTENCE WASN'T MISGUIDED.

BUT IT DOES NOTHING TO CONVINCE ME.

PROFESSOR YODOGAWA WOULD CERTAINLY VIEW THIS...

THEN WHY DID YOU KEEP ALL THIS STUFF?

I'M TRYING TO BECOME A PROPER BIOLOGIST.

YOU MUST BELIEVE IN PERSISTENCE TOO.

HE EVEN DREW SKETCHES OF HIS IMAGINARY CREATURE...

...AND MADE NOTES ON ITS CHARACTER-ISTICS AND WEAKNESSES.

THERE'S NOTHING HERE BUT AN OLD MAN'S *DELUSIONS!*

YOU DON'T KNOW ANYTHING ABOUT BIOLOGY.

LET'S FIND THAT STUFF!

NO, IT'S NOT.

IT'S CHILDISH NONSENSE.

I'VE BEEN LOOKING THROUGH YODOGAWA'S NOTES AND...

...AN OLD FRIEND NAMED SHO!

I HAVE...

SO WHAT?

122

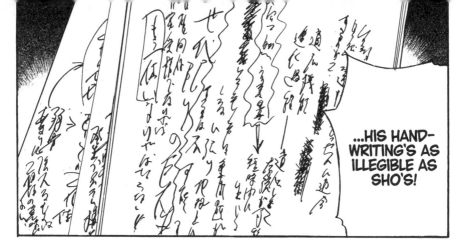

...HIS HAND-WRITING'S AS ILLEGIBLE AS SHO'S!

MY HANDWRITING IS SO BAD I CAN'T WRITE YOU...

ASA!

I'M RACING KOKICHI TSUBURAYA...

...TO TELL YOU I'M FINE!

...AND I'M BLOWING PAST HIM!

IDIOT! YOU GOT A DEATH WISH?!

!!

AW, MAN...

S-SORRY!

DUMB KID!

THANKS FOR THE RACE, KOKICHI TSUBURAYA!

I...

I...

HEH HEH...

WHEN DID YOU TAKE UP RUNNING, YATARO ISHIDA?

HEY.

HELLO.

I'M JUST MIMICKING HIM!

...THE OLYMPIC RUNNER KOKICHI TSUBURAYA!

FROM A DISTANCE YOU LOOKED LIKE...

WELL, STICK WITH IT.

HEH HEH...

I...

I'M GONNA DO THIS!

...ASA!

JUST YOU WATCH...

ASADORA!

ASADORA!

Chapter 22 ◉ Just a Fighter Plane

Chofu Airfield, Tokyo
October 6, 1964

MISTER
KASUGA!!

WHAT'RE YOU YELPIN' ABOUT?

HEY, MISTER!!

WHAT'D YOU DO TO HER?!

...BEHIND MY BACK?!

WHAT'D YOU DO TO HER...

IF YOU WANT INSTANT RAMEN, MAKE IT YOURSELF.

WHO'S "HER"?

SLURRRP

WHAT'S THAT CANNON THING?!

THESE ARE 70-MILLIMETER MK 4 FFAR ROCKETS. EACH ONE WEIGHS ABOUT 10 KILOGRAMS.

IT ISN'T A CANNON. IT'S A ROCKET LAUNCHER.

ROCKET LAUNCH-ER?

...

YEAH. FOR THESE.

Chapter 22 ◎ Just a Fighter Plane

TO KEEP FROM EXCEEDING THE CUB'S MAX CARGO CAPACITY, THE ROCKETS WOULD USUALLY NEED TO BE 9 KILOGRAMS EACH...

...BUT THAT'S ASSUMING TWO PASSENGERS WHO WEIGH 70 KILOGRAMS EACH.

YOU'RE LIGHT, SO IT'S FINE.

NO, IT'S *NOT* FINE!

NO, THAT'S NOT TRUE.

IT WENT QUITE WELL.

SHE ISN'T SUITED FOR SHOOTING ROCKETS!

YOU... SHOT ONE?

YEAH, AS A TEST.

WHAT DO YOU MEAN?

HUH ?

...AT THE EAST FUJI MANEUVER AREA.

I ATTACHED THE LAUNCHER LAST NIGHT AND SHOT ONE THIS MORNING...

134

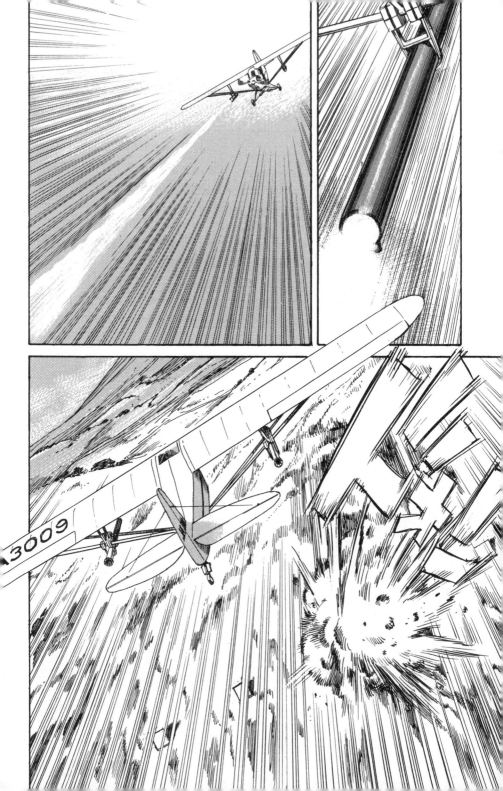

...BUT WE MIGHT TAKE DAMAGE FROM THE BLAST OR THE RESULTING DEBRIS.

THE CUB IS SLOW, SO WE CAN GET IN CLOSE BEFORE FIRING...

...

I'M SO SORRY, GIRL...

YOU'RE NOT ITS MOTHER.

YOU SHOULDN'T HAVE DONE THIS!

YOU AND I BOTH SAW THAT THING.

DO YOU REALLY WANT TO FACE IT UNARMED?

EVEN NOW, I HAVE NIGHTMARES.

IF WORSE COMES TO WORST, THIS AIRCRAFT MUST ACT AS...

...A FIGHTER PLANE.

THAT SCHOLAR GUY WILL FIND A WAY TO FIGHT THAT THING IN HIS MENTOR'S WRITINGS.

A FIGHTER PLANE?

URRRGH...

I TOLD THEM I'D DECIPHER THIS, BUT...

ARGH!

SKRITCH SKRITCH SKRITCH SKRITCH SKRITCH

...I CAN'T READ IT!

...WE'LL SHOOT IT WITH A ROCKET.

IF HE FINDS THAT THING'S WEAK SPOT...

...

YOU'RE FREE TO DECLINE TO PARTICIPATE.

IF THE MEDIA FOUND OUT ABOUT AN ARMED CIVILIAN PLANE...

DON'T TELL ANYONE ABOUT THIS.

AND ONE MORE THING.

...A FIGHTER PLANE.

RIGHT NOW SHE'S JUST...

SO SHE'S CURRENTLY GROUNDED FOR ALL OTHER PURPOSES.

...IT'D BE THE END OF US.

IS THAT... TRUE?

SIGH.

SLURRRP

I'M IM-PRESSED.

SLURRRP

NO, THAT WAS NOTHING.

...SINCE I SAW YOU FLY.

IT'S BEEN A WHILE...

143

BUT YOU MANAGED A DEAD HIT WITHOUT SIGHTS OR A SCOPE.

MY RIGHT HAND IS HOLDING ME BACK.

NO...

YOU HAVEN'T LOST YOUR SKILL.

IS YOUR PUPIL BETTER?

ANYWAY, THANKS TO THE PAY FOR THIS JOB, WE WON'T LOSE THE COMPANY OR THE PLANE.

WELL...

NO.

144

THANK YOU.

THE SUCCESS OF THE OLYMPICS IS WORTH ANY PRICE.

IF YOU NEED MORE, SAY THE WORD.

NO MATTER WHAT OCCURS, WE HOPE FOR YOUR SAFETY.

BUT ANYTHING MIGHT HAPPEN.

WELL, I'M GRATEFUL FOR THAT, BUT...

HOPE?

...HOPE DOESN'T MEAN THINGS WILL GO WELL.

YES?

...THAT I MIND.

NOT...

I'M PREPARED FOR ANYTHING.

THE GOVERNMENT AND SDF AREN'T INVOLVED.

AND THAT'S WHY WE ARE.

LIKE YOU SAID, ANYTHING MIGHT HAPPEN.

...THE TYPHOON WAS HARD ON ASA.

BUT AS I SAID BEFORE...

NOT TO MENTION, WE WITNESSED SOMETHING THAT SEEMED OTHERWORLDLY.

SHE LOST HER FAMILY, AND IN THE FIVE YEARS SINCE...

SHE FEELS A CONNECTION TO THAT THING.

...I'VE WATCHED HER GROW UP.

...THERE'S NO WAY TO REMOVE HER FROM THE MISSION.

...NOW THAT SHE KNOWS ABOUT THIS...

...BUT...

I DON'T WANT TO EXPOSE HER TO DANGER...

SO I NEED TO ASK A FAVOR.

148

...BUT...

I KNOW THIS HAS TO GO OFF PERFECTLY...

...PUT THE BLAME ON ME!

...IF SHE CAUSES ANY TROUBLE...

AS IF I DID IT ALL MYSELF!

NO ONE CAN KNOW SHE WAS ON THAT PLANE!

TNK

FWSH

RRIP

PUFF

PUFF
PUFF

YES?

HEY.

OKAY, THANKS.

I MADE YOU RAMEN.

WHAT'S WRONG?

ASADORA!

OH...

SPLOSH

KOSHICHI! WHAT'RE YOU DOING?! YOU'RE SOAKING WET!

YOU WERE SUPPOSED TO WAIT AT KINDER-GARTEN!

DID SOME-ONE HIT YOU?

NO.

D-DID SOME-THING HAPPEN?!

YOU'RE MISSING A RAIN BOOT!

NO. CHIKO'S LITTLE BROTHER YASUBE.

EITHER WAY, THIS MEANS TROUBLE.

YOU BEAT UP YASUBE?

WAS IT CHIKO AGAIN?

YOU DID? WHO?

CRUMPLE

WHY'D YOU DO THAT?

I DREW THIS, AND HE SAID IT WASN'T REAL.

?!

*PAPER: KOSHICHI ASADA

SO I CAN DRAW IT OVER AND OVER.

I SAW A KAIJU.

KOSHICHI...

OH, THAT AGAIN?

...BUT THAT WAS THE DAY YOU WERE BORN.

YOU SAID YOU SAW IT RISE OUT OF THE OCEAN...

BUT *I* DID!

...BUT NO ONE ELSE SAW IT.

I KNOW YOU BELIEVE YOU SAW ONE...

MAYBE *YOU* SHOULD APOLOGIZE THIS TIME.

THAT WAS JUST A DREAM!

···

KOSHI-CHI!

NO WAY!

HUH?!

...AND THAT MEANS WE'RE ALL LIARS!

YASUBE SAID OUR MOM ISN'T OUR REAL MOM...

AND SHE LOOKS DIFFERENT! AND SHE'S SUPER OLD!

THAT AIN'T YOUR MOM! HER LAST NAME'S DIFFERENT!

...

YOU PUNCHED OUR LITTLE BRO!

I'M BACK FROM SCHOOL...

...BUT I SHOULD GO PICK UP KO-SHICHI.

HAZUKI AND SHINROKU ALREADY WENT.

WHERE HAVE YOU BEEN GOING AFTER SCHOOL? YOU'RE ALWAYS LATE.

RATTLE

SORRY! I'VE BEEN DOING RESEARCH!

I'LL GET RIGHT TO WORK!

...

W...

WHAT HAPPENED ?!

WITH WHO?!

CHIKO AGAIN?!

WE GOT IN A FIGHT.

!!

YOU IDIOTS!!

...AND KEKO'S OLDER BROTHER KOJI AND YUJI AND SEJI!

YEAH! CHIKO AND KEKO...

KOSHICHI DREW THAT WEIRD PICTURE AGAIN!

WHAT STARTED IT?!

WHEN WILL YOU EVER LEARN?!

...

REALLY?

I DIDN'T.

PSST PSST

YOU SHOULDN'T HAVE TOLD KOSHICHI!

ISN'T THAT WHAT YOU SAW DURING THE TYPHOON?

AND SAID YOU AREN'T OUR REAL MOM!

THEN THEY CALLED US LIARS!

BUT KOSHICHI ALWAYS DRAWS THIS.

I DIDN'T TELL ANY OF THEM.

WHO SAID THAT?

HE CALLED YOU "SUPER OLD."

YA-SUBE.

OOPS.

YOU SHOULDN'T HAVE SAID THAT...

YOU CHILDREN WAIT HERE.

KINUYO! YOU NEED AN UMBRELLA!

UH, YEAH.

THE TAMADA FAMILY NEAR THE TOFU PLACE?

Chofu Airfield

YOU REALLY SHOULDN'T HAVE SAID THAT...

168

RATTLE RATTLE

SPLOSH

SPLOSH

CRIK

GAH!!

WHAT WERE YOU LOOKIN' AT?

HUH?

I W-WAS JUST, UM..

...LOOKING FOR MIKAWA AIR TRANSPORT'S HANGAR.

IT'S BACK THAT WAY.

OH...

UH, THANKS!

*COAT: DAILY EVERY NEWSPAPER COMPANY

A REPORTER, HUH?

日刊エヴリー新聞社

HELLO IN THERE!

BAM BAM

HELLO?

NOK NOK

!!

RATTLE

WHERE'S YOUR MOM?

SHE'S AT WORK.

WHICH OF YOU ARE YASUBE, CHIKO, KEKO AND KOJI?!

ARE YOU YASUBE?

I'M SORRY.

KOSHICHI HIT YOU.

173

...YOU SHOULDN'T CALL PEOPLE LIARS.

BUT...

...

...

AFTER ALL, WHAT KOSHICHI DREW MAY BE REAL.

AND YOU WERE WRONG TO SAY...

THE WORLD HOLDS MANY MYSTERIES ...

...SO THINK TWICE BEFORE YOU SPEAK.

...I'M NOT THEIR REAL MOTHER.

WE'RE EVERY BIT AS CLOSE AS BLOOD.

BUT YOU WERE RIGHT ABOUT ONE THING.

...

YOU CAN CALL ME A YOUNG LADY.

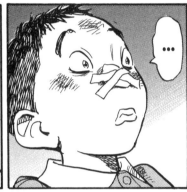

I'M NOT YOUNG ANYMORE.

IT'S OKAY TO LIE ABOUT THAT.

...

SLAM

SO BE GRATEFUL!!

YOUR PARENTS ARE THE REAL THING TOO WITH SO MANY MOUTHS TO FEED.

YOU SAID THAT THING TOOK YOUR FAMILY.

DO YOU BELIEVE ME?

JUST LIKE MINE WAS.

WHAT A BIG FAMILY.

...YOU'D BE DEAD SET ON FIGHTING IT TO GET YOUR FAMILY BACK.

WELL, IF IT REALLY EXISTS...

BECAUSE YOU'RE IMPORTANT TO ME.

...

BUT I'D STOP YOU.

...

AYE, THIS RAIN ISN'T GONNA LET UP!

THE WAVES ARE HIGH. SHALL WE TURN BACK?

WHAT'S WRONG?

HM?

Sagami Bay

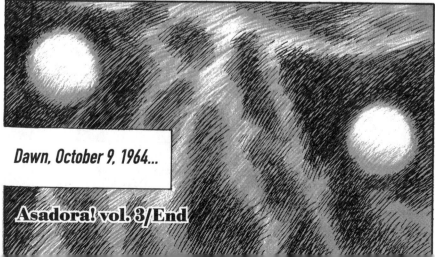

Dawn, October 9, 1964...

Asadora! vol. 3/End

ASADORA!

To be continued...

Production Staff:

Hideaki Urano

Tohru Sakata

Cooperation:

Satoshi Akatsuka (TAC Photography)

Jun Takahashi

Yorimasa Takeda

Hidetaka Shiba

Nagoya Times, Archives Committee

Japan Aeronautic Association, Aviation Library

Hajime Matsubara (The University Museum, The University of Tokyo)

National Museum of Nature and Science

Takeshi Ijichi (Ikaros Publications, Ltd.)

Akatsuka

Satomi Danno

Editor:

Haruka Ikegawa

References:

Takahashi, Jun. *Jun-san no Ozora Jinsei, Oreryu* (Jun's Life in the Skies, My Way).
Assisted by Masahiro Kaneda. Ikaros Publications, Ltd.

Takeda, Yorimasa. *Blue Impulse: Ozora o Kakeru Samurai-tachi*
(Blue Impulse: Samurai Who Fly Across the Sky). (Bungeishunju Ltd.)

Thank you to everyone else who offered help.

PAGE 107: *Uiro* is a chewy, subtly sweet Japanese steamed cake comprised of sugar and rice flour. It comes in a variety of flavors, such as red bean paste, strawberry, green tea, yuzu and chestnut. Nagoya, in particular, is famous for its uiro.

PAGE 112: Kokichi Tsuburaya was a Japanese athlete who competed in the marathon and the 10,000-meters event at the 1964 Tokyo Olympic Games. Tsuburaya took sixth place in the 10,000 meters and was in position to take second in the marathon until Britain's Basil Heatley overtook him suddenly in the final lap. Tsuburaya placed third in the event. Ashamed of his performance, Tsuburaya vowed to make amends to the people of Japan by running and hoisting his home country's flag in the next Olympic Games in Mexico. Unfortunately, after the Tokyo Games, Tsuburaya wound up suffering from lumbago, which made it nearly impossible for him to train. Tragically, in 1968, Tsuburaya died by suicide in his dorm room while training for the Mexico City Olympics. In his hand was his bronze medal from the Tokyo Games.

PAGE 116: Kenji Kimihara is a retired Japanese long-distance runner. He competed in the 1964 Olympics alongside Kokichi Tsuburaya, placing eighth. He also competed in the 1968 and 1972 Olympics, where he finished in second and fifth respectively. Kimihara had a number of first-place finishes outside of the Olympics, such as in the 1966 Boston Marathon and the 1966 and 1970 Asian Games. In 2016, to celebrate the 50th anniversary of his Boston Marathon win, Kimihara ran the marathon again, finishing with a time of 4:53:14.

PAGE 116: Toru Terasawa is a former Japanese long-distance runner who finished 15th in the marathon at the 1964 Olympics. On February 17, 1963, Terasawa set a marathon world record with a time of 2:15:16 at the Beppu Marathon.

PAGE 134: The East Fuji Maneuver Area serves as the major training grounds for the Japan Ground Self-Defense Force on the island of Honshu in Japan.

Translation Notes

PAGE 19: The bullet train railway project began in Japan in 1959. Just five years later, the Hikari bullet train opened to the public on October 1, 1964. The train, which traveled between Tokyo Station and Shin-Osaka Station, was the fastest on the line. It made fewer stops than the slower Kodama, making the Hikari the premier train of the time. These 0 series models remained in use until 1999. Today, the Hikari bullet trains operate on the Tokaido and Sanyo lines.

PAGE 34: Blue Impulse is the Japan Air Self-Defense Force's aerobatic demonstration team. The team's formation was inspired by the 1959 visit of the Thunderbirds, the United States Air Force's air demonstration squadron. The official Blue Impulse team was founded in 1960 at Hamamatsu Air Base as a team of five F-86 Sabres. In 1964, at the Tokyo Olympic Games, Blue Impulse successfully drew the Olympic rings in the air with colored smoke. The squadron continues to put on airshows for awestruck crowds to this day.

PAGE 64: Due to its affordability, simplicity and popularity, the Piper J-3 Cub is considered by many to be the Ford Model T of aircraft. The light American aircraft was produced by Piper Aircraft between 1938 and 1947. Despite being designed as a trainer, the Cub also gained popularity as a general aviation aircraft and proved well suited for a variety of military missions, including reconnaissance, liaison and ground control. In fact, during World War II, it was mass produced as the L-4 Grasshopper. Following the war, many L-4s were civilian-registered under the designation J-3.

PAGE 80: *Shabondama Holiday* (Soap Bubble Holiday) was a Japanese music variety show hosted by twin pop-sensation duo the Peanuts from 1961–1972. The Japanese jazz band and comedy group Hajime Hana and the Crazy Cats costarred on the show. A number of celebrities appeared on the show during its 11-year run.

PAGE 82: The Western Carnival was a rock music festival that began in Japan in the 1950s at Nihon Gekijo (also known as Nichigeki Theater) in Tokyo. The now-defunct rock festival was Japan's first.

Sound Effects Glossary

The sound effects in this edition of *Asadora!* have been preserved in their original Japanese format. To avoid additional lettering cluttering up the panels, a list of the sound effects is provided here. Each sound effect is listed by page and panel number; for example, "6.3" would mean the effect appears in panel 3 of page 6.

8.3 - hwip (bi: taking photograph)

11.2 - hwup (ba: taking documents)

11.6 - fwump (dosa: loading documents)

18.7 - honk honk honk
(paaa pappaa puaa: vehicles honking)

19.1 - honk honk (paaa pappaa:
vehicles honking)

20.6 - munch munch munch
(hagu hagu hagu: eating)

21.1 - hwonk (puan: train horn)

22.5 - skrik (zaa: jeep stopping)

24.3 - vreeeee (kiiiiin: jets flying)

25.1-3 - hwooosh (gooooooon: jets flying)

26.2 - swooosh (kiiiin: jets flying)

34.4 - hrooosh (kiiiin: jets flying)

38.1 - vreeen (kiiiin: jet landing)

38.2 - vrshhh (goo: jet landing)

39.5 - fwip (ba: saluting)

44.6 - fwap (pan: swatting)

59.6 - vroosh (kiiiin: jet flying)

60.1 - gwoosh (goooo: jets flying)

78.4 - slam (batan: closing car door)

86.8 - tunk (bamu: closing car door)

87.1 - vroom (vuo: car leaving)

87.4 - vroom (baa: car)

88.1 - vroom (vuoo: car)

90.6 - gwap (ga: grabbing)

100.1 - creak (gii: door opening)

103.1 - fump (dosa: setting down newspapers)

105.2 - hup (ta: starting to run)

109.3 - shtmp (da: stopping)

112.4 - whsh (da: running)

114.1 - woosh (da: running)

119.1 - whoosh (da: running)

124.1 - fwoosh (da: running)

124.2 - honk (paaa: truck horn)

124.5 - vroom (baa: truck leaving)

129.1-2 - vrrrr (buuuuu: airplane flying)

130.1 - bam (ban: bursting in)

131.4 - bam (ban: bursting in)

134.7 - vrrr (buuuu: airplane engine)

135.1-5 - vrrrrr (buuuuuu: airplane flying)

136.3 - boom (doon: explosion)

137.1 - bwoom (ooon: explosion)

155.1 - tshhhhh (zaaaaa: rain)

155.2 - tshhhhh (zaaaaa: rain)

158.7 - hwup (ba: raising paper)

160.1 - vrrr (buun: airplane flying)

163.2 - thok (pan: punching)

171.2 - tshhhhh (zaaaaa: rain)

172.1-4 - yaaaaaaah
(waaaaaaaaa: commotion)

173.1 - bump (do: colliding)

177.4 - sloosh (zaan: parting waves)

ASADORA!

Volume 3
VIZ Signature Edition

By Naoki URASAWA/N WOOD STUDIO

Translation & Adaptation John Werry
Touch-up Art & Lettering Steve Dutro
Design Jimmy Presler
Editor Karla Clark

ASADORA! Vol. 3
by Naoki URASAWA/N WOOD STUDIO
© 2019 Naoki URASAWA/N WOOD STUDIO
All rights reserved.
Original Japanese edition published by SHOGAKUKAN.
English translation rights in the United States of America, Canada,
the United Kingdom, Ireland, Australia and New Zealand arranged with SHOGAKUKAN.

Original Cover Design: Isao YOSHIMURA + Bay Bridge Studio

Printed in Canada

Published by VIZ Media, LLC
P.O. Box 77010
San Francisco, CA 94107

10 9 8 7 6 5 4 3 2 1
First printing, July 2021

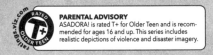

 MEDIA 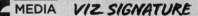 VIZ SIGNATURE

viz.com   vizsignature.com

This is the last page.

Asadora! has been printed in the original Japanese format
to preserve the orientation of the artwork.